Golf Sv  Instruction

Understand the Fundamentals of a Golf Swing Such as Posure, Grip and Control to Achieve Range, Accuracy and to Improve Your Game as a Whole

By Haydon McMillen

© **Copyright 2019 - All rights reserved.**

The content contained within this book may not be reproduced, duplicated or transmitted without direct written permission from the author or the publisher.

Under no circumstances will any blame or legal responsibility be held against the publisher or author for any damages, reparation, or monetary loss due to the information contained within this book. Either directly or indirectly.

Legal Notice:

This book is copyright protected. This book is only for personal use. You cannot amend, distribute, sell, use, quote or paraphrase any part, or the content within this book, without the consent of the author or publisher.

Disclaimer Notice:

Please note the information contained within this document is for educational and entertainment purposes only. All effort has been executed to present accurate, up to date and reliable, complete information. No warranties of any kind are declared or implied. Readers acknowledge that the author is not engaging in the rendering of legal, financial, medical or professional advice. The content within this book has been derived from various sources. Please consult a licensed professional before attempting any techniques outlined in this book.

By reading this document, the reader agrees that under no

circumstances is the author responsible for any losses, direct or indirect, which are incurred as a result of the use of information contained within this document, including, but not limited to, —errors, omissions, or inaccuracies.

Contents

Introduction 1
Chapter 1: The Ball 4
Chapter 2: Using the Iron 9
    Purchasing a Driver or Fairway Wood 12
    Purchasing the Proper Fairway Woods 15
    Picking the Right Irons 16
    Wedges 17
    Which Iron to Utilize 18
Chapter 3: Stance 20
    The Ideal Posture 22
    Golf Club Grip 24
Chapter 4: The Swing 27
    Common Issues with a Swing 35
Chapter 5: Power Driving 39
Chapter 6: Repairing the Slice 48
Conclusion 55

Thank you for buying this book and I hope that you will find it useful. If you will want to share your thoughts on this book, you can do so by leaving a review on the Amazon page, it helps me out a lot.

Introduction

As a golfer, you understand how lousy it could be when you are striking the ball too short for every drive. It could cost you the game and result in a truly lousy score. In case you want to find out how to hit the ball more at every hole, you have to go through this guide.

The goal of this guide is to show you how you may enhance your shot to grant you more than 50 yards each time you hit the golf ball. There are a great deal of elements that need to be taken into consideration as you play golf.

These elements consist of the kind of ball you are utilizing, your position, swing, power driving, and obviously, how to repair your slice. Only one of these elements being off could lead you to have less drive.

This guide ought to be utilized to aid you to comprehend how you ought to correctly stand as you hold your club. You are going to discover how the club must be facing to achieve particular shots, how to strike across the tree, down the fairway and out of the sand with total power. You are going to likewise discover where to place the weight in your body during the whole swing.

You may be giving everything you have actually got and still are not able to hit the ball as far as you would wish. You may believe you have to lift weights and develop your arm muscles.

The strength in your shot isn't about the strength of your arms. It has to do with the appropriate ingredients of swing, stance, the manner in which you hold the club, and far more.

When you have just the appropriate swing, you are going to discover you are able to drive the ball as far as you want to as you golf. You could get the extra range you are searching for when you understand how to make the crucial components work.

Those extra yards are going to suggest less par and a much better rating. You are going to be astonished with the enhancements in your game.

Chapter 1: The Ball

You may have an incredible swing; however, it will not do anything for you if you aren't utilizing the appropriate golf ball. There is no reason to be squandering an ideal swing if you are not utilizing the appropriate ball.

When you are playing golf with the appropriate golf ball, it could take a couple of strokes. There are numerous methods to tell which kind of golf ball you have to utilize as you play the game. These likewise are going to make a huge distinction with the range you get as you strike the ball.

There are 3 various kinds of golf balls. These 3 various golf balls are referred to as two-piece, balata, or a ball with the mix of both of the two. There are numerous things you have to think about as you are picking which of these balls you are going to utilize.

The initial thing you have to consider is what you are searching for. Do you wish to have the supreme spin control while having a low handicap? The balata is for you. This is a softer ball that has a softcover. The softcover enables the ball to have a tad more of a spin. The pro golf players utilize the Balata as they golf, involving Tiger Woods.

In case you are searching for more range in your swing and you have a greater handicap, then you require more control over the durability and range. This indicates you require a hardcover ball. A two-piece ball consists of a hardcover which are not going to develop as much backspin. By doing this, you are going to have the ability to hit the ball a further range than you have previously.

As you select a ball to utilize as you are playing golf the weather condition might play into your choice also. You likewise wish to take a look at the golf course conditions. In case the course has actually been drenched in the rain, the ball which is going to produce the least amount of spin and is going to go further is going to be your finest option.

In case the golf course is scorched from the sun and rock solid then the softer ball is going to be the ideal option. This is due to the fact that the softer ball is going to land gently and spin as opposed to bouncing.

The half and half ball has a bit of both the hard and soft mixed. You may attempt this ball if the conditions appear to be just proper and you require a bit of range; however, you are dealing with the spin control as well. Striking with the various balls is going to provide you an excellent idea of the distinction they make as you play the game.

Another method to tell what ball you want to select additionally depends upon the swing. In case you have a fairly sluggish golf swing, then you must think about the two-piece ball. Range is important and with a slow swing, you require a ball which is going to assist you to travel further. As you are on the greens the downside is going to be that the ball is not going to spin a lot as you work closer towards the hole.

A few of the balls you may think about for the two-piece include the Pinnacle Platinum Feel, Nike Juice, and the Titleist DT Carry & Roll. You could locate a three-piece ball which provides the identical advantages as the two-piece balls referred to as the Top-Flite Gamer.

Golf players with a swing, that is a tour like are going to swing 110 miles per hour and more. These players have the capability to compress their long irons and drives. They normally benefit more from utilizing the softer ball.

A few of these golf players utilize a three and even a four-piece ball, that permits them to produce around the greens effortlessly. This classification of a ball could be found as the Bridgestone Tour B330 Series, Callaway Tour series, Nike One series, Titleist Pro V1, TaylorMade TP, and more.

When selecting a golf ball, you must think about a couple of things. You might lack range in your play due to the fact that you are utilizing the incorrect kind of ball. The softer and more pricey golf balls are for the pros who are able to swing the club over 100 miles per hour.

You may believe the most pricey is always the greatest; however, if you are not one of the top dogs they are not going to assist you. The ideal balls for a sluggish swinger are the less expensive two-piece golf balls. They are going to aid you add range to each long shot.

Chapter 2: Using the Iron

There are numerous things which have to be thought about when you pick a golf club set. These things involve how to select the proper golf club set. You want to understand the distinctions between the various kinds of clubs, the components, and more.

Comprehending these things could aid you make a more suitable choice in which clubs are right for you. You likewise have to understand how to utilize your irons that involves various positions and more.

The initial thing you require is a fundamental set of clubs. There is no reason to bring more than 14 clubs in your bag at once and it is really against USGA policy in case you do. Your bag ought to consist of 2 or 3 woods, 2 fairway woods and a driver, 8 irons, and extra wedges. In case you desire a putter, these are typically sold individually.

The iron shaft could make all of the distinction in how far you can hit the ball. There are 2 main kinds of shafts that include graphite and steel.

Steel shafts are sturdy, offer more resilience, and they are less expensive clubs. A set of clubs with steel shafts are going to offer better consistency from every shaft. You may even have greater shot control.

The important thing about steel shafts to keep in mind is that they are ideal for golf players with a quicker swing. If you wish to produce a great range with these kinds of shafts, you ought to be a strong golf player who is trying to find control in your game.

Graphite is lighter than steel and is really made in numerous variations. These clubs are more costly and they are not as resilient as steel. Due to the light-weight, the graphite shafts enable a quicker swing, that leads to a tad more power.

You may be compromising a little bit of control as you swing the club due to the speed. Graphite clubs are likewise much better if you wish to soak up the shock sent to your wrist from the club after impact. Gloves likewise assist with this.

Another thing to search for is a thing referred to as flex. This is the shaft bend, additionally referred to as the whip. The shaft bend needs to match the a golf swing speed. A flexible shaft is ideal for a newbie golf player who has a less strong and slower swing.

The typical golf player has a swing around 75 miles per hour to 90 miles per hour, which calls for a regular shaft. A firm or stiff shaft ought to be utilized for golf players who have a swing over 90 miles per hour. The stiffer the golf clubs are, the more control the player has with the ball.

Nowadays there is a shaft referred to as the uniflex which is created to match any kind of swing.

Purchasing a Driver or Fairway Wood

Selecting the appropriate fairway and driver wood could be tough if you do not understand how huge the clubhead size ought to be. Here are a couple of pointers.

When you are selecting a wood, there are 3 various clubhead sizes to select from. The basic clubhead size measures roughly 150-155 cubic centimeters. This size has a tinier sweet spot but is going to provide you greater control.

The midsize size measures around 195 cubic centimeters and provides a couple of advantages. This is going to provide you a medium-sized sweet spot and the club is additionally a lot lighter than the club head which is oversized.

The oversized clubhead is the largest you could pick from. The clubhead could be located at sizes up to 300 cubic centimeters. This provides a huge sweet spot with any of the head sizes. This is a lot more challenging for you to manage and is more heavy than the other 2 versions.

The clubhead comes in 2 materials. These materials can just make a distinction with how they feel and how they appear. These materials are titanium and stainless steel. They likewise vary in cost substantially.

Stainless steel is a lot heavier and cheaper than titanium. The appearance of a stainless steel club is more conventional and feels like that as well. The head is tinier due to the heavyweight.

The titanium is a lot lighter and enables the club to have a bigger clubhead. There is a bigger sweet spot and the club appears to be a lot more forgiving than the standard stainless steel versions.

The clubface head loft makes a huge difference in how far you may hit the ball. You have to understand how to select the club loft if you wish to add more range.

Loft is the measurement of the clubface head angle. The greater the loft measurement is, the higher the angle is going to be on the clubhead face. This is going to permit more control of the ball yet less range in your shot. The less clubface loft, the greater the range. The more range you have, the less control over the ball you are going to have.

Your swing is going to additionally make a distinction with the kind of loft you require with your clubs. If you have a sluggish swing, you desire the highest loft. This suggests you are going to try to find clubs with a loft between 10.5 and 12 degrees.

If you are a typical golf player with a typical swing, then you have to locate a loft between 9.5 and 10.5.

The experts have the quickest swings and they are going to have the lowest loft at about 8 to 9.5. In case you are swinging over 90 miles per hour you may desire this loft as well.

Purchasing the Proper Fairway Woods

Lots of golf players feel more comfy as they are standing over a long fairway with a lower profile and longer wood instead of a long iron which is tougher to strike.

It is simpler to get the ball in the air out of the fairway in case you have a lower center of mass. This is additionally correct if you are in the sand or in the rough.

You could make the most of more range without needing to overswing when you have a bigger club rather than a long iron. You could additionally have more control with the length.

Lots of folks are substituting their long irons with fairway woods. If you wish to attempt to utilize wood instead of iron for these advantages of range and control, you may wish to think about these couple of things.

Picking the Right Irons

The irons are utilized for shorter golf shots. These may vary from 200 yards and even less than 100 yards.

The capability of the player to strike the distance and the clubhead loft are going to be the determining factors for selecting the best iron. There are 2 main kinds of irons that involve the forged and the cast irons.

The cast irons have a cavity back construction that is additionally referred to as perimeter weighting. The head weight is primarily around the exterior. The cast irons have a bigger sweet spot due to the fact that more weight is placed around the clubface edges. These irons are ideal for novices who miss the ball and they are additionally more forgiving as opposed to the forged irons.

There actually isn't a weight distribution which happens with the forged irons on the clubhead back. The center of gravity happens in the clubhead middle. An advanced player could utilize a forged iron for greater trajectory due to the weight being higher in the face. This iron enables more precision when you have actually missed hits.

Irons have the identical kinds of club heads as the woods and they are additionally created with stainless steel and titanium. The less sophisticated players must play with the stainless steel irons due to the provided consistency and sturdiness.

Wedges

There are 4 various kinds of wedges. Wedges are utilized to get yourself out of a difficult spot and often, it might call for a little bit of a range. The various kinds of wedges entail the sand wedge, pitching wedge, lob wedge and gap wedge.

The pitching wedge is utilized for longer wedge shots from 125 yards. The sand wedge is utilized for the sand.

The gap wedge is thought about as a compromise between the pitching and the sand wedge.

Which Iron to Utilize

As you are utilizing an iron, there are various factors to consider based upon how you have to hit the ball. There are 3 irons you need to understand that entail the long iron, the mid-iron and the short iron.

When you utilize a short iron the ball is going to remain in the center of the stance and the club is going to be somewhat behind it. The best ball position is in the center of your stance.

The peak of your swing ought to be a couple of balls forward. This implies that you are going to hit the ball at a steep angle, generating a large divot. Your feet are going to be nearer to the ball than they are going to be as you utilize a long iron.

The mid-sized iron is utilized a bit differently. The ball is not going to be right in the center of your stance but it is going to be somewhat forward. The longer the iron is, the more forward the ball is going to have to be. You are going to still hit the ball with a tough blow; however, not as steep as you require with the short iron. The divot is going to additionally not be as deep as well.

When you utilize a long iron the ball is going to be furthest from you. You wish to hit the ball in a sweeping motion instead of striking down on the ball. The ideal method to hit the ball is at the apex of your swing arc.

There is no requirement to force the ball up by striking the ball on the upswing. The ball is going to immediately end up being airborne due to the angle of how you strike the ball.

Chapter 3: Stance

How you stand could make a huge distinction in how you hit the ball. It can additionally determine the range of your shot. Your Swing is key. How you have your feet, where you are looking, and even how you move your bodyweight all enter into play as you strike the ball.

Your stance is really crucial when you plan to hit the ball. There are 3 various stances you ought to understand that include open, square, and closed. Something to think about is that it is generally ideal to utilize the identical stance as the same clubface positioning.

For instance, if you are utilizing an open stance then you must utilize an open clubface. Never ever move the clubface angle in a position which opposes how you are standing.

When you utilize a stance which is square to the ball's target line, you are going to impact the club to swing down the line a tad longer than when you would if your stance is closed or open.

In case you were to gauge where the majority of golf players were, in fact, aiming, you would notice the square stance is most frequently utilized. An closed or open stance is going to really make the shoulders follow through correctly.

An open stance must be utilized as you are moving the ball from left to right. As you utilize an open stance you are going to align your stance slightly open. Your shoulders are going to swing the club across the ball. The broader your legs are, the more open your stance is. The more open, the broader your shoulders are going to be additionally.

An open stance is a great option for somebody who has a tendency to overswing on the ball. The trajectory and the curvature of your shot additionally depend upon the amount you turn the clubface as you address the ball. As you open the clubface, you receive a shorter shot and a high trajectory.

A closed stance is the ideal as you are moving the ball from right to left. That suggests your stance is somewhat close to the ball target line.

As your stance is closed, your shoulders swing the club from your body's interior. A closed stance is the most effective option as you are attempting to pick up the range on your swing. These shots are going to have less height but travel more.

The Ideal Posture

There are a couple of things you want to do so as to have excellent posture as you are getting ready to strike the ball.

If you wish to strike the ball properly and get the range, you require to stand effectively with the best posture. If you do not have the ideal posture there is going to have to be some kind of compensation in your swing if you wish to set the ball on the proper course.

You need to have a completely flat back as you are standing. Flatten your back up versus your iron and make certain it is flat. This is going to aid with your posture.

As you hold the club and move, you want to bend from the hips. Bend from the hips as you bring the club to the head and back. In case you are somebody who rounds their shoulders or keeps straight legs, the club is not going to have the ability to stay in place.

You need to bend your knees in an athletic position. Bend your knees into place like you were playing baseball waiting for somebody to hit the ball towards you.

Now your legs are bent and you have a flat back. The angle between your club and your chest ought to be at a 90-degree angle. Your club shaft and your belt ought to likewise be on the identical plane. You could look at your posture in a mirror in case you are uncertain if you have the best stance.

Golf Club Grip

There are 3 various kinds of grips as you hold a golf club. Not everybody utilizes the identical grip. As you are utilizing the appropriate golf club grip, it is going to feel natural and really comfy to you.

There are particular basics that you ought to utilize so as to have the appropriate golf grip. The various kinds of golf grips consist of the interlocking, overlap and the ten-finger.

The overlap grip is the most typical grip for the majority of players. This grip ended up being well-known around the turn of the 20th century. This is additionally the most typical grip shown by instructors for newbies also. The club is, in fact, held in the fingers.

To utilize the overlap grip you are going to lay the club in your fingers with your pinkie finger opened. The thumb is going to fit on the lead hand which is grasped around the club. The lead hand's thumb is going to fit in the trailing hand's lifeline. If you are a right-handed player, your lead hand is going to be your left hand.

The interlocking grip is the following most typical grip. This grip is well-known with expert golf players. This grip interlocks the hands together. There is danger associated with this grip since the stray might lead to the palms. This type of grip is chosen by the majority of folks who have weak lower arms and wrists, little hands, and novices.

As you wish to utilize the interlocking grip, you are going to take the little finger on the trailing hand (in case you are left-handed, left hand is your trailing hand) and intertwine it with the forefinger of the lead hand or the left hand. The lead hand thumb is going to fit into of the right or trailing hand lifeline.

The ten-finger grip is likewise called the baseball grip since you are going to hold the club like a baseball bat. This is the favorite amongst the golf trainers.

There are benefits to this kind of grip. Trainers choose this grip due to the fact that it makes instruction simple. When learning the interlocking grip, it could be complicated and cause issues. This is a standard grip and easy to do. Somebody who experiences joint discomfort, weak hands, arthritis, and other issues might choose this kind of grip.

When you utilize the ten-finger grip, you are going to place your hands correctly beginning with the grip of lead hand. Put your little finger versus the trailing hand forefinger. Both hands are going to grasp the club securely and be pushed up versus one another.

Chapter 4: The Swing

There are numerous elements to an excellent swing. You could have excellent shoes, balls, clubs, and these things are not going to matter in case you have a poor swing. If you wish to include range to your shot, you have to concentrate on your swing with every single shot.

Numerous golf players devote years attempting to perfect their swing. This could be a life-long and tough goal. Concentrating on a couple of basic things could help you lessen any odds of slicing the ball, missing the ball, and not getting the range you are attempting to attain. This is going to lead to fewer strokes being needed to get the ball to the hole on each run.

The most crucial thing is your posture. Make certain you have exceptional posture prior to hitting the ball. Line up the club straight ahead of you as you stand with your rear completely straight. Your left arm ought to additionally be straight and extended. You must be comfy in this position.

It is essential to bear in mind that this swing is created for a right-handed golf player. When a right-handed golf player remains in this stance and practicing this swing, a left-handed golf player could stand straight ahead of this person and appear as if you are standing in the mirror to attain the identical outcomes.

You are going to raise your left shoulder as you are lowering the right one. You are not going to place your weight on the right foot or lean to the right. Make certain your stance stays straight upward as you vertically raise and lower your shoulders. As you are dropping the right shoulder, your right arm is going to be tapping your stomach's lower right side.

With this form, you are going to make sure you are in the appropriate beginning posture. This is going to likewise be nearly the identical posture when the club makes contact with the ball. Thinking about this position aids you to minimize any chance of missing the ball or leading to a bad strike.

The plane is the area which encompasses the body, stomach and chest. This is your following focus. You want to see 3 points; the area where your arm and stomach touch, the handle, and your right hip's far side. These 3 aspects are the swing plane.

As you swing your club, you are going to pull it back flexing your right elbow, somewhat keeping a straight left arm. The clubface is going to, in fact, be above your head. As you come down in your downswing, this is where the velocity and the force of the swing enter into play, and it is a really essential element of the swing.

Make sure you forcefully come down on the shot as you stretch the right arm. Your weight is going to, in fact, move to your right leg. You are going to follow through with the club as you make contact with the ball.

Your left arm must be utilized to direct the swing as well. Your upper body is going to turn towards the fairway as you would be watching the ball in the air. During the follow-through, your left arm is going to be bent and your right arm is going to be straight.

Practicing your swing is extremely crucial. There are lots of reasons why your swing might be the cause of inadequate range. You do not need to be striking a ball to practice your swing.

Nevertheless, you could devote hours at a driving range practicing your swing with the various kinds of clubs.

Practice is key when it pertains to the swing. If you do not understand how to swing the club effectively then you might never do it right.

Your hands ought to stay low in the swing follow-through. The higher your hands are, the more trajectory you are going to have in the ball. The importance is range. You wish for the ball flight to stay low.

It is additionally essential to be certain you are on the plane on top of your swing. If you wish to ensure precision and a strong strike, you should be on plane when you reach the clubface at the top of your swing. Your right forearm ought to be parallel to your spinal column.

Your left wrist ought to be flat and your arms and elbows are going to form a tight triangle. When these elements are there, you are going to ,likewise, make sure you turn your shoulders correctly in the backswing.

Your body supplies the power when you utilize it effectively. You do not get your power from your arms. So as to utilize your body correctly, you are going to place the club behind the ball at address. Your body is going to assume a dead-stop position.

You can't move the ball in this position easily. As you utilize the club with your body, you are going to discover that you are able to get the ball in the air more regularly. On your downswing, you are going to likewise rotate completely.

You likewise have to gain control over your swing's length if you desire strong contact with the ball. The club shaft and left arm ought to have a 45-degree angle upon setup. This is going to begin the swing with the wrists hinged midway to the 90-degree angle you require to be at.

In the takeaway, the hands are going to stay near to the ground as the clubhead goes upward rapidly. The objective is to have the left thumb pointed down at the right shoulder as rapidly as you are able to.

You could tell if you accomplish this effectively is by taking a look at your left arm. It needs to be parallel to the ground and the club shaft ought to be perpendicular to it as well. You are going to hinge your wrists in the backswing and this is going to lead to a consistent direction and distance on all of your iron shots regardless of the range.

Portion of your swing has to concentrate on the tilt of the right elbow and the shoulder. You want to be certain you don'thave a faulty shoulder which causes you to slice the ball. The ideal position for the right elbow is within the seam running down the shirt's right side.

When your elbow stays in your shirt's seam, this is going to enable the shoulders to turn level to your spinal column. This is going to make it simple to drop the club within during the downswing, and that is going to lead to optimal power and as much control as feasible.

In case you have a strong plane, you are not going to slice the ball. This is an element which could aid to avoid the slice anyhow. At the point of contact, you wish to make certain you do not have an open face. The swing course typically has a tendency to come too much on the outside, which could lead to issues with your direction and contact. Each golf enthusiast's swing course should come from within.

During your backswing, it is essential to bear in mind not to stiffen your leg. In case you do stiffen the back leg, you are going to tilt out of balance. This is going to make it tough to rebend the knee upon the ball impact.

Lots of golf players call the angle you create in your back leg by the lower and upper leg the special K. The angle ought to be preserved from the initial moment to after the impact so as to preserve a level swing. The ideal method to practice the special K is to swing in the mirror and see your position.

As you are setting up the special K, your body is going to appear as you are in a position which is prepared for action. At the address, you are going to bend your back knee during the swing. All your body needs to do is turn if you are prepared properly. Your lower leg has to be straight down and up. This special K stance opens your hips so they may turn appropriately.

Upon impact, the arm which trails has to snap directly to launch the power into the ball. The back knee is going to kick towards the target while staying in the special K flex. After impact, both your arms are going to be straight and the clubhead is going to be beneath the hands. The club butt ought to be pointed towards the center of the body.

You are going to likewise preserve the special K position during the backswing. This is going to enable your elbows to stay level close to the swing top. This is going to lead to stopping the clubface from twisting out of the position you require it to be in.

Utilizing the special K position of the backswing is going to assist the club shaft in traveling along the appropriate swing course as you slowly acquire power as the club rises to the target.

Common Issues with a Swing

There are numerous factors in a swing which could cause you to lose range with your shot. These things could be simple to repair if you are able to recognize what you are doing improperly with your swing. Here are several things you may do with your swing which could be fixed.

A reverse pivot happens as you rotate your body too much and you do not move the weight from your left front foot. This is going to make you lunge behind the ball and in fact, scoop it. This is called a fat shot. You may even pop the ball up accidentally as you carry this out.

If you wish to prevent a reverse pivot, you will need to handle your weight appropriately when you swing the club. The majority of your body mass needs to move to your back foot throughout your backswing.

You need to bear in mind that sliding and shifting aren't the identical things. An appropriate weight shift happens as you turn. The body is going to turn away and the weight is going to naturally shift to the rear foot.

Turning is a huge element when it pertains to power. As you move and turn, you are loading your rear leg with torque. This places you in the ideal spot to come down fast and hard on the downswing. As you turn appropriately, you are going to unwind quicker and strike the ball harder.

You could likewise lose range in your shot when you have a late wrist cock. This could likewise lead to swaying. This element of a swing is the most neglected but is extremely common.

As you cock your wrist correctly, it could, in fact, aid you to turn your body better. This is going to likewise increase the ball speed. You need to set your wrist earlier. As soon as your hands reach the waist, they need to remain in the 90-degree angle. Your left arm is going to be straight as your right elbow still tucked into your side.

This is going to offer an effective rotation as you swing. The wrist cock likewise aids you to avoid dipping your shoulder as well. The appropriate wrist cock makes it possible for you to swing with a level shoulder plane.

When you launch prematurely, you could likewise lose power in your shot. Releasing your hands prematurely is a misconception lots of amateur golf players believe is the appropriate thing to do. You are in danger of losing your club as well. The source of this might be from an overactive right hand.

The ideal way to stay away from an issue of launching the club too rapidly is to turn your body before launching the hands. It is about rotating the body.

Chapter 5: Power Driving

Driving is among the essential elements you have to dominate when playing golf. You want to be able to have a power drive to strike the ball directly and with range.

Many individuals have a difficult time striking the ball far and discover that this is where they include additional strokes into their play. If you might just strike the golf ball a bit more, then you would have a much better game. There are lots of ways in which you could concentrate on your drive to make your game more effective and satisfying.

Handling your drive is really crucial. You want to concentrate on your strengths straight off of the tee. This is going to aid you to be a much better player. If you understand how you typically hit the ball, you could attempt altering your drive to utilize it.

For instance, if you discover that you usually hit the ball and the ball flight generally curves to the left, then you may wish to stand close to the right side of the tee. This could aid to make up for a left curve.

There are 2 things that need to be thought about when you wish to hit the ball long. These things consist of increased clubhead speed and making strong contact with the golf ball.

If you are able to acquire the capability to swing the club regularly on the identical swing plane while keeping the clubface control, you are going to have the ability to make solid contact. Snapping the hips through the ball during the contact is going to likewise aid with boosting the speed.

The most effective way to strike with a rising blow is to tee the ball well forward in your stance. Never ever enable roll. Your wrist must not break down and your arms have to be totally extended. This is going to produce a broad arc for your club.

Your shoulders need to be turning around your body. Never ever position excessive weight at your body's front. Make certain to move your weight effectively during the swing.

The incorrect hip rotation could lead you to lose power during the swing. Many golf players move their hips laterally instead of turning them counterclockwise.

When performing a lateral slide, it is going to create an issue which can lead to hook or a slice which is going to lead to an absence of power. You could likewise injure your back.

Correct motion of the hips is important to the stroke power. As the hips are more open than the shoulders when the club is delivered is the most effective method to store power and deliver it straight into the impact.

Additionally, when the hips are cleared it is going to assist to keep the correct spinal column angle during the impact. This is going to encourage the best weight shift for strong contact.

A great drive needs power and overall control. When attempting to attain control and power you have to correctly launch the club via impact. You likewise need a powerful left to right ball flight. The appropriate method to do this is to shift your club and arms left after the impact.

If you are attempting to attain a shot which is lower moving left to right, you wish to move your hands to the left instantly after impact. Keep the shaft angled. Your lower arms are not going to turn upon impact and the clubface is going to stay somewhat opened.

If you wish to attain a right to left ball flight, you wish to enable the clubhead to pass your hands after the golf ball impact. This is going to enable an inside attack. You wish to attain transferring more power to the ball than you usually do, which is going to aid you to get a higher right to left stroke.

Setup is important to offering your drive additional power. You should establish your swing appropriately. You must utilize a wood or a driving iron to appropriately establish your drive due to the club length. Utilizing a longer club is going to provide you with 2 benefits.

You are going to have the ability to boost the range of your stance far from the ball and this is going to likewise enable you to spread your feet more. This is going to enable you to stabilize your weight as you move it in your swing. By doing this, you could get a brief yet wider swing, which is going to enable overall power and control ,which is all going to have the appropriate percentages.

The sequence of movements is really essential to comprehend in your swing and your setup. The sequence ought to be in order from establishing, swinging, and driving as you utilize the appropriate weight transfer.

This is really difficult for amateur players but it is necessary to preserve the sequence. Establishing your game in this sequence could aid with a more effective strike.

Your power has to accumulate completely and then be launched totally upon impact. Building power starts in the swing. Constantly launch your power as you make an impact with the ball. The swing has to stay brief.

You are going to have less control over your strike the longer your swing is. Lots of newbies believe that you need to swing long to strike far. A wide and brief swing is going to deliver the most control and power over your strike.

Preserving a balance is really crucial. To achieve this, you need to swing within yourself. As you swing, make certain you do not swing too much forward or back. Make certain to stay within yourself so you remain in control. This is going to aid you uniformly disperse your weight from heel to toe.

You should make certain to preserve excellent posture, maintain your spinal column lined up straight and your chin must be upright. These things are going to aid you prevent injury and knock the ball down the fairway with strength.

Keep in mind when you drive the ball you do not ever have to swing as much as you can as if you are playing baseball. You may have the identical kind of swing yet be swinging in a different swing plane.

Nevertheless, you do not require huge muscles to make the golf ball go far.

Lots of great golf players are extremely thin and they have the capability to strike at very long ranges. It is all about leverage. As soon as you master the leverage, you are going to have the ability to add the range to your shots as well.

Concentrate on the angle you produce between your left hand and the club. This angle has to be held as long as possible. In case you force yourself to hold this angle, it might lead to a bad swing. Certain golf players see club as a whip.

Among the ideal ways to produce the leverage is to start the downswing with a shift of your hips towards the target. This is going to aid to develop the power you are storing so you are able to launch it on the impact with the ball.

You additionally have to be certain to swing inside your limits and absolutely nothing more. When you swing as hard as you are able to, it is ridiculous.

Concentrate on your swing and make certain to swing as freely as you are able to with control.

If you discover that you frequently lose balance with your swing, then you are probably swinging too forcefully.

When you swing the golf club conveniently instead of stretching or swinging too forcefully, you are going to have the ability to attain more range by releasing the ball with the appropriate trajectory and spin. This is the most effective method for you to strike the ball as far as you are able to and straight.

Your focus ought to be on precision, and after time your range is going to improve, likewise.

On the golf course, you can not be out there practicing. In other words, do not concentrate on the mechanics. You should have practiced the mechanics sufficiently to be in a position to believe in your swing now.

If you are able to believe in your swing, you are going to have the ability to swing more effectivelly and strike the ball with a more strong strike. Releasing the ball with great trajectory and spin takes place when you believe in your swing.

Chapter 6: Repairing the Slice

A golf slice could be ravaging and extremely discouraging to a golf player. There are numerous elements that might cause you to slice the ball. If you discover you slice the ball on a regular basis, then you are going to have to repair it.

If you wish to enhance your general game and include range to your shots, picture how far the ball would go if you might simply straighten out your shot.

A golf slice happens as your club is open upon the club effect and relative to the clubhead course.

A wayward left hand is among the typical elements which can cause you to slice the ball far to the right. This takes place more frequently than you would believe. When a wayward left hand takes place, the back of your left hand is going to be lined up to the right of the ball and the clubface is going to be open. This is going to result in a slice to occur.

If you wish to fix a wayward left hand, it is necessary to concentrate on the rear of your hand. The rear of your hand ought to be encountering the target at impact. You need to at least sense that the rear of your hand is facing your target. This is going to enable you to have a powerful grip to ensure your hand does not slip.

It is necessary to square your left hand. Among the ideal methods to do this is by practicing without utilizing a club whatsoever. You are going to stand with your right arm to the side and turn your left forearm. Then you are going to cock your left wrist and swing back.

A weak grip is a typical element and reason for a wayward left hand, resulting in the ball slicing far in one direction, generally the right. A weak grip is going to result in you turning your hands too much to the left. You may have a square backhand and discover that you are still slicing the ball. This is frequent when it comes to golf players with an extremely weak grip.

You need to tighten your grip as you swing as hard as you can on a long drive. You may repair this additionally by rotating your hands to the right on the club as you are keeping a great position while holding a club.

Among the important things to bear in mind is that when you concentrate on preserving a strong grip, you are going to likewise have a tough time with how you turn the club. This is due to the fact that it is really simple to turn your left hand over. This is going to make it simpler, so you do not need to go far for the club to be square. However, it is an incorrect position.

You need to have one thing in mind as you are trying to keep the ideal grip and square. In case you are trying to square your left hand and you discover that you are unable to, it is going suggest something else.

Even though you are attempting to repair your slice, you are searching in the incorrect location. Not having the ability to fix the slice by squaring your wrists could suggest that something is wrong with your swing rather than the grip.

An additional thing which may cause you to slice the ball is having an excessive amount of a steep plane in your swing. This could certainly make ball head in the direction you didn't want it to go in.

Swinging the ball too steep makes it far too hard for your hands to have the capability to turn over. This likewise indicates you are going to be incapable of turning over and squaring your club with the ball impact.

In case you have a really steep plane in your swing and the propensity to slice the ball due to this, then you could repair it. This kind of swing is a natural repercussion of things which make you strike downward. Do not hit the ball downward. That is what results in the slice.

If you are a golf player who swings the club dirrectly up and after that directly down, it is going to cause you to obstruct the open face. It is important to swing the club around the body like you are using a baseball club.

You may even act like you are swinging a baseball club outward. Now, take the club and imagine your baseball is on the floor. You are just altering the swing plane as you swing your club against the baseball bat. Lots of instructors are going to teach you this, and you could attempt it. This is a great method for amateur golf players to attempt due to the fact that it truly aids.

The shoulder tilt is one more thing which could result in you slicing the ball. In case you have an awkward slice, then you want to take a look at how you are moving your shoulders. The issue is not originating from your arms going up and down.

When a shoulder tilt happens, the body is not rotating and tilting as it is ought to. Your arms have nothing to do with it. If you want to fix a shoulder tilt, you wish to swing the arms around the body.

One method to do the swing properly is to place your arms around your chest and rotate in pivot back and forth. When you have your shoulder swing down, then you could put a club in your hands and practice swinging correctly.

Certain players have a truly excellent golf swing. They take a look at all of the aspects and can not find out what is triggering the issue. The last thing you wish to take a look at is if you are turning the clubface excessively when it is moved far from the ball. This occurs frequently and it makes you open the club face too much, and after that, you have a further range to square the ball once more upon impact.

It is necessary to be certain the club is square in your backswing. In case you are not sure where to verify this during the swing, inspect your club when your swing is at 2 o'clock. The club ought to be square as you are holding the club like this.

An issue slicing the ball could originate from various elements. Every action of a swing might have an issue which might cause you to slice the ball. The method to identify what is leading to your slice is to have a look at your whole swing from how you are grasping the club, opening the clubface, moving the weight, and more. You may even discover something wrong that is going to aid you further.

Fixing a slice in the golf game could make a huge distinction to the score at the end of the round. Not just are you going to get a significant range with the shot, but you are going to have struck a straight ball. This implies you will not have to hit the ball once again only to recover it out of the sand.

Conclusion

Including power to your game and range to your shots does not indicate you have to do a bit of arm strengthening and bodybuilding. There are numerous elements which could remove range when you golf. When you comprehend these things, you could include greater ranges to your shots each game.

The club you utilize is considerably based upon how good you swing the club. This likewise depends upon your swing speed and more. You need to think about the materials, shafts and more when you select a club set.

You can not utilize your buddy's clubs and hope to have a great game. An excellent club set ought to be determined and measured and your convenience factor.

The kind of ball you utilize to golf is going to be identified by how you swing the clubs as well. You want to identify the course conditions and the weather as well. These things are going to likewise make a distinction with the kind of ball you pick and obtaining the most range from your shot.

A lot of the other elements you have to think about so as to include more range to your shot each single time you play golf involve your weight shift, your stance, your swing, shoulders, wrists, and more.

There are numerous elements to your swing, and in case you lack range, you have to take a look at how you are accumulating and moving the power to the ball on impact.

Fixing mistakes in how you play could aid you to add range to your game. You may be utilizing the incorrect kind of club or ball, or simply have to correct your slice. You may do these things when you understand which elements to search for.

I hope that you enjoyed reading through this book and that you have found it useful. If you want to share your thoughts on this book, you can do so by leaving a review on the Amazon page. Have a great rest of the day.

Printed in Great Britain
by Amazon